Cake Mix
COOKING *for* KIDS

D1294308

Cake Mix
COOKING *for* KIDS

Stephanie Ashcraft

Photographs by Zac Williams

GIBBS SMITH
TO ENRICH AND INSPIRE HUMANKIND

Manufactured in Shenzhen, China in July 2011 by Toppan Printing Company

First Edition
15 14 13 12 11   5 4 3 2 1

The cooking and baking activities suggested in this book may involve the use of sharp objects and hot surfaces. Parental guidance is recommended. The author and publisher disclaim all responsibility of injury resulting from the performance of any activities listed in this book. Readers assume all legal responsibility for their actions.

Published by
Gibbs Smith
P.O. Box 667
Layton, Utah 84041

1.800.835.4993 orders
www.gibbs-smith.com

Designed by Rita Sowins / Sowins Design
Gibbs Smith books are printed on either recycled, 100% post-consumer waste, FSC-certified papers or on paper produced from sustainable PEFC-certified forest/controlled wood source. Learn more at www.pefc.org.

Library of Congress Cataloging-in-Publication Data

Ashcraft, Stephanie.
  Cake mix cooking for kids / Stephanie Ashcraft ; photographs by Zac Williams. — 1st ed.
     p. cm.
  ISBN 978-1-4236-1917-8
  1. Baking. 2. Quick and easy cooking. I. Title.
  TX763.A773 2011
  641.8'15—dc22
                        2010052248

To my children—Devan, Elizabeth, Spencer, and Emma. You are my life, and I love each one of you more than you'll ever know.

see recipe on page 33

Getting
Started

Welcome, young chefs, to the world of baking! There are a few things you need to know before you get started on your baking adventure.

General Kitchen Rules

* Always get permission from an adult to use the kitchen. Plan ahead. Read and reread the recipe several times. Make sure you have all the ingredients before you start.

* Wash your hands with soap and water before starting your baking adventure. Continue to wash hands after cracking eggs, handling dough, or touching the trash can.

* Wear close-fitting sleeves that won't accidentally catch fire.

* Get out all of the kitchen tools needed before beginning your project: pans, cookie scoops, bowls, spatulas, oven mittens, measuring cups, and whatever else may be required.

* For best results, follow the recipe exactly.

* Always use oven mittens or pot holders when putting food in or taking it out of the oven. I suggest you always have an adult assist you in placing and removing items from the oven to avoid getting burned.

* Knives are not toys. Always have an adult assist you when you are cutting anything with a sharp knife. Keep your fingers away from the blades of sharp knives.

* Clean as you go. Throw away wrapping and packaging as soon as you are done using the product inside. Wash dishes as you are done with them.

* Turn off burners or oven when you are finished.

Kitchen Tools Needed

* Glass or metal bowls for mixing and holding ingredients
* Set of measuring cups
* Set of measuring spoons
* Rubber or plastic spatula
* Metal spatula
* Knives for cutting
* Butter knives or spatula for frosting
* Cutting board
* Ice cream scoop
* Metal or wooden spoons for stirring or scooping
* Cookie scoops—1 tablespoon size (small), 2 tablespoon size (medium), and 3 tablespoon size (large)

* Rolling pin
* Rotary beater
* Baking sheets
* Mini muffin pan
* Muffin pan
* 9 x 13-inch pan
* Cupcake liners
* Oven mittens or hot pads
* Cooling rack
* Powdered sugar shaker
* Wax paper
* Plastic wrap

Glossary of Terms

Bake — to cook food in an oven.

Beat — using a mixer, rotary beater, or whisk, stir rapidly until ingredients are well mixed.

Chill — to cool in the refrigerator.

Combine — to mix ingredients together.

Cool — to allow warm/hot baked goods to sit at room temperature until no longer warm.

Fold — use a spatula to gently mix ingredients together by cutting down the bottom of the bowl with the spatula, sliding it under the mixture, and bringing it back up. Repeat.

Knead — to push, fold, and turn dough on a counter or other flat surface.

Mix — to stir ingredients together so the mixture looks the same all over.

Preheat oven — set oven to indicated temperature before baking.

Measuring and Mixing Tips

* Measuring flour and sugar—stir flour or sugar in the storage container or bag. Using a large spoon, lightly spoon flour or sugar from the container into the measuring cup. Do not shake the cup and do not pack the flour or sugar. However, if you are measuring brown sugar, you do need to pack the brown sugar in the measuring cup. Using the back of a table knife, level off the flour or sugar even with the top edge of the measuring cup.

* Measuring seasonings—using a measuring spoon, scoop and then level using the back of a table knife.

* Measuring butter—a stick of butter has measuring amounts marked on the sides of the paper wrapping. Just cut where you need to and unwrap the butter.

* Do not over mix the batter when making cupcakes or cakes.

* When making cookie dough, mix until all dry ingredients are worked completely into the dough.

Baking and Cooling Tips

* Always preheat your oven to the correct temperature before baking. When the oven reaches the set temperature, you can place the item to be baked inside. Set timer for the lowest time mentioned on recipe. Bake longer if necessary.

* Bake cookies and bars until the edges start to turn a light golden brown color. Remove and allow cookies to cool on the pan for 5–10 minutes. Use a spatula to place cookies on cooling racks.

* Check cakes by inserting a clean toothpick in the center of the cake. If it comes out clean, the cake is done. If not, return cake to oven and bake a couple more minutes. Test again.

* Place baked items on cooling rack while still in the pan, for at least 10 minutes, before attempting to remove from the pan.

* Allow cookies, cakes, and cupcakes to cool to room temperature before frosting and decorating or the frosting will melt and slide off.

* Cut the baked recipe into bars or squares when completely cool unless the recipe specifies differently. This helps prevent the bars from crumbling.

* Store baked items in a tightly covered container or leave them in the pan and cover tightly with aluminum foil. This prevents the treats from drying out. Storing leftovers in the refrigerator will keep items fresh longer.

* Store baked items made with cream cheese, milk, pudding, or whipped topping in the refrigerator before and after serving.

Sweetheart
Sprinkle Cookies

MAKES 23–25 COOKIES

1 cherry chip or
    strawberry cake mix

2 eggs

⅓ cup canola oil

½ cup flour

1 container (16 ounces)
    white frosting

assorted pink sprinkles
    and/or heart shaped
    candies

Preheat oven to 350 degrees. Mix together cake mix, eggs, and oil in a large bowl until cookie dough is formed. Stir in flour and work into dough by hand if needed. Roll half of dough onto a nonstick cutting board until ¼-inch thick. Using a cookie cutter, cut out heart-shaped cookies. Repeat with other half of dough.

Place heart cookies on a baking sheet that has been prepared with nonstick cooking spray. Bake 10–12 minutes, or until slightly golden around the edges. Allow cookies to completely cool on a cooling rack. Frost cooled cookies with frosting and decorate with pink sprinkles and/or heart candies.

Little Lemon Sandwich Cookies

1 lemon cake mix
2 eggs
⅓ cup canola oil

½ cup powdered sugar
1 container (16 ounces)
   cream cheese frosting

Preheat oven to 350 degrees. Mix together cake mix, eggs, and oil in a large bowl until cookie dough is formed. Place powdered sugar in a small bowl. Drop 1 tablespoon cookie dough into powdered sugar. Roll the ball of dough in the powdered sugar and place it on a baking sheet that has been prepared with nonstick cooking spray. Place 12 balls of dough on each baking sheet.

Bake for 8–12 minutes until cookies turn a light golden brown on the edges. Remove cookies from oven. Using a spatula, remove cookies from baking sheet and place them on a cooling rack to cool. Once they are completely cooled, spread a layer of frosting in between two cookies to make sandwich cookies.

Chocolate Chip
Oatmeal Cookies

1 spice or vanilla cake
   mix

2 eggs

$\frac{1}{3}$ cup canola oil

$\frac{1}{3}$ cup applesauce

2 cups quick oats

1 cup chocolate chips

Preheat oven to 350 degrees. In a large bowl, use a spoon or fork to mix together cake mix, eggs, oil, and applesauce. Stir in oats 1 cup at a time and then add chocolate chips. Drop 1-inch balls of dough onto a baking sheet that has been lightly prepared with nonstick cooking spray. Bake for 9–12 minutes, or until lightly golden brown around the edges. Remove cookies from baking sheet and place on a cooling rack to cool.

Simple Snickerdoodles

1 white cake mix
2 eggs
$\frac{1}{3}$ cup canola oil

1 teaspoon vanilla
2 teaspoons cinnamon
$\frac{1}{2}$ cup sugar

Preheat oven to 375 degrees. Mix together cake mix, eggs, oil, and vanilla in a large bowl until dough is formed. In a small bowl, combine cinnamon and sugar. Drop cookie dough 1 tablespoon at a time into cinnamon-sugar mixture. Roll dough until completely coated. Place balls of dough onto a baking sheet prepared with nonstick cooking spray. Bake for 8–10 minutes, or until lightly golden brown around the edges. Place cookies on a cooling rack to cool.

Black Owl
Cookies

¾ cup creamy peanut
　butter

2 eggs

⅓ cup water

1 chocolate cake mix

¼ cup sugar

plain M&Ms

Red Hots

Preheat oven to 350 degrees. Beat peanut butter, eggs, and water together in a large bowl until smooth. Gradually stir in cake mix until cookie dough is formed. Drop 2 tablespoon-size balls of dough onto a baking sheet prepared with nonstick cooking spray. Place sugar in a small bowl. Flatten ball of dough with the bottom of a glass that has been dipped in sugar. Pinch out 2 ears at top of cookie and the chin at the bottom of the cookie. Add M&Ms as eyes and a Red Hot or a sideways M&M of a different color as a nose. Bake 9–11 minutes. Place cookies on a cooling rack to cool.

Mini
Cookie Cups

MAKES 46–48 MINI COOKIE CUPS

1 yellow cake mix

2 eggs

⅓ cup canola oil

46 to 48 miniature peanut butter cups or Rolo candies

Preheat oven to 350 degrees. Mix together cake mix, eggs, and oil in a large bowl until cookie dough is formed. Prepare a mini muffin pan with nonstick cooking spray. Drop 1 tablespoon dough in each mini muffin cup. Completely unwrap candies and throw away all wrappers. Press 1 candy into the center of each dough cup, allowing the dough to rise up sides until ¼ of candy remains visible. Bake for 10–12 minutes. Allow cookie cups to cool in the pan. Remove and place on a platter to serve.

PEANUT BUTTER VARIATION: Stir ½ cup creamy peanut butter into cookie dough.

DIFFERENT CANDY VARIATIONS: Bite-size Snickers can also be used, or 1½ cups M&Ms or Reese's Pieces can be stirred into the dough and baked as cookie cups.

Candy
Cookie Pops

½ cup butter or margarine

1 white cake mix

2 eggs

½ cup flour

18 paper sucker sticks

1 package (16 ounces) vanilla CANDIQUIK coating

red or blue food coloring

sprinkles or small round candies

Preheat oven to 350 degrees. Melt butter in a medium micro-waveable bowl in the microwave for 30 seconds. Stir until most of the butter is melted. Pour cake mix over butter and make an indentation in the middle. Crack eggs into indentation and stir until dough forms. Add flour and knead into dough by hand.

Using a medium cookie scoop, place 6 balls of dough per baking sheet that has been prepared with nonstick cooking spray. Place a sucker stick into each ball so that the stick is horizontal to the baking sheet. Bake for 10–12 minutes. Remove and allow cookies to completely cool. Place cookie pops in the freezer for 1 hour.

Melt CANDIQUIK according to package directions and stir in 3 drops of food coloring. Dip top half of cookies in melted coating, immediately decorate with sprinkles, and place on wax paper to cool. Allow coating to completely harden before serving.

Pink Pudding
Bars

1 strawberry cake mix

2 eggs

1/3 cup canola oil

1 cup white chocolate
 chips

Topping

1 box (3 ounces) vanilla
 or white chocolate
 instant pudding

1 1/2 cups milk

red food coloring

sliced strawberries

Preheat oven to 350 degrees. Mix cake mix, eggs, and oil together in a large bowl. Stir white chocolate chips into dough. Lightly prepare a 9 x 13-inch pan with nonstick cooking spray. Spread dough evenly into pan. Bake 14–18 minutes or until lightly golden brown around edges. Using a wooden spoon handle, immediately poke holes in bars 1 inch apart from each other.

In a separate large bowl, beat pudding mix and milk together with a wire whisk for 2 minutes. Drop 2 to 3 drops of red food coloring into pudding and whisk until it becomes a uniform pink color. Pour 1/2 of the pudding over warm bars. Place the rest of the pudding in the refrigerator and chill for 5–10 minutes. Frost bars with remaining pudding. Cut into 24 bars and store in refrigerator. Just before serving, place strawberry slices over top of each bar.

Brownie
Bites

½ cup butter or
   margarine

1 chocolate cake mix, any
   variety

2 eggs

2 tablespoons water

1 teaspoon vanilla

1 cup chocolate chips*

powdered sugar

Preheat oven to 350 degrees. Melt butter in a large microwave-able bowl in the microwave for 30 seconds. Stir until most of the butter is melted. Pour cake mix over butter. Make an indentation in the middle of the cake mix and add the eggs, water, and vanilla. Stir until dough forms and then add chocolate chips into the dough.

Prepare a 9 x 13-inch pan with nonstick cooking spray. Spread dough into pan and bake for 20–25 minutes. Allow brownies to completely cool. Shake powdered sugar over the top using a powdered-sugar shaker. Cut into bite-size pieces.

* You can use mint chocolate chips, peanut butter chips, or white chocolate chips as well.

NUTTY BROWNIE BITES: Stir in ¾ cup chopped walnuts or pecans in place of chocolate chips.

CAKE-LIKE BROWNIE BITES: Stir in ¼ cup water instead of 2 tablespoons water.

Peanut Butter
Bars

1 yellow cake mix
1 cup peanut butter
1 egg
$\frac{1}{3}$ cup water

Topping
1 container (16 ounces)
    chocolate frosting
$\frac{1}{2}$ cup peanut butter
chopped peanuts or
    chopped peanut butter
    cups

Preheat oven to 350 degrees. In a large bowl, stir together cake mix, 1 cup peanut butter, egg, and water until dough is formed. Spread dough into a 9 x 13-inch pan that has been prepared with nonstick cooking spray. Bake for 17–20 minutes. Allow bars to completely cool.

In a medium bowl, combine chocolate frosting and $\frac{1}{2}$ cup peanut butter. Frost bars and then cut into 24 bars. Top with peanuts or peanut butter cups.

Super Brownie
Sundaes

½ cup butter or
   margarine

1 chocolate cake mix, any
   variety

2 eggs

2 tablespoons water

1 teaspoon vanilla

vanilla ice cream

1 bottle (20 ounces)
   caramel syrup

1 can (7 ounces) whipped
   cream

chocolate sprinkles

Preheat oven to 350 degrees. Melt butter in a large microwave-able bowl in the microwave for 30 seconds. Stir until most of the butter is melted. Pour cake mix over butter. Make an indentation in the middle of the cake mix and add the eggs, water, and vanilla. Stir until dough forms. Using a paper towel, spread a thin layer of shortening around the inside of each cup in two 12-cup muffin pans. Scoop about 2 tablespoons of dough into each muffin cup. Bake for 12–15 minutes.

Remove from oven and allow brownies to cool for 5 minutes. Top individual brownies with 1 scoop of ice cream. Drizzle caramel over ice cream and decorate the top with whipped cream and chocolate sprinkles.

Vanilla
Blondies

1 box (3 ounces) instant vanilla pudding mix

2 cups milk

1 teaspoon vanilla

1 vanilla or white cake mix

1⅔ cups white chocolate chips

1 container (16 ounces) vanilla frosting

assorted colored sugars, sprinkles, or sugar candy decorations

Preheat oven to 350 degrees. In a large bowl, whisk together pudding mix and milk according to package directions. Whisk vanilla into pudding and refrigerate for 5 minutes. Stir cake mix into the pudding mixture until blended. Stir in white chocolate chips. Spread batter onto a baking sheet with sides that has been prepared with nonstick cooking spray. Bake for 30–35 minutes. Allow blondies to cool. Spread frosting over top and decorate with colored sugars, sprinkles, or sugar candy decorations.

Bubblegum
Bars

1 confetti or rainbow chip
   cake mix
2 eggs
⅓ cup canola oil

1 container (16 ounces)
   white frosting
assorted sprinkles
24 gumballs

Preheat oven to 350 degrees. Mix together cake mix, eggs, and oil in a large bowl until dough is formed. Spread the dough evenly into a 9 x 13-inch pan that has been lightly prepared with nonstick cooking spray. Bake for 14–17 minutes until edges are a light golden brown. Allow bars to cool completely in the pan. Frost and cut into 24 bars. Decorate with sprinkles and place a gumball in the center of each decorated bar.

Cookies-and-Cream Cupcakes

1 white cake mix
$1\frac{1}{4}$ cups water
$\frac{1}{3}$ cup canola oil
3 eggs
$1\frac{1}{2}$ cups crushed Oreo
cookies

Frosting
1 container (16 ounces)
vanilla or white
frosting
$\frac{1}{2}$ cup crushed Oreo
cookies

Preheat oven to 350 degrees. In large bowl, mix together cake mix, water, oil, and eggs until smooth. Gently stir in $1\frac{1}{2}$ cups cookies. Insert cupcake liners into two 12-cup muffin pans. Spoon 3 tablespoons batter into each cup of the pans. Bake for 16–20 minutes. Cool completely.

Mix together frosting and $\frac{1}{2}$ cup cookies. Decorate cupcakes with frosting and additional cookie crumbs, if desired.

Mini Cupcake Kabobs

1 strawberry or
   pineapple cake mix
ingredients listed on the
   back of box
20 hulled strawberries

1 can (20 ounces)
   pineapple chunks
2 to 3 bananas, peeled
   and cut into chunks
20 wooden skewer sticks

Preheat oven to 350 degrees. Prepare cake mix according to package directions. Prepare mini muffin pan with nonstick cooking spray. Place 1 tablespoon batter into each cup. Bake for 10–12 minutes until golden around edges. Allow to cool for 5 minutes before removing to cooling rack where the cupcakes can completely cool. Repeat process with remaining batter. You will have 80–84 mini cupcakes when you are done.

On each wooden skewer, thread cupcake, banana chunk, cupcake, strawberry, cupcake, pineapple chunk, and a final cupcake.

Banana Bread
Cupcakes

1 spice or vanilla cake mix

ingredients listed on back of box

3 ripe bananas

1 teaspoon baking soda

Frosting

1 box (3.4 ounces) instant banana cream pudding mix

1 cup milk

1 container (8 ounces) whipped topping, thawed

Preheat oven to 350 degrees. In a large bowl, prepare cake mix according to package directions. Peel bananas and mash them in a separate bowl. Stir baking soda into bananas until well blended. Mix bananas into the batter. Line two 12-cup muffin pans with cupcake liners. Fill each liner with 3 tablespoons of cake batter. Bake for 20–24 minutes. Allow cupcakes to cool.

In a large bowl, mix together the pudding mix and milk until completely smooth and thick. Fold whipped topping into pudding to combine. Spread frosting over cupcakes. Chill until ready to serve. Refrigerate any leftovers.

VARIATIONS: Stir in ¾ cup mini chocolate chips into the batter if desired. Cheesecake or vanilla flavored instant pudding can be used in place of banana cream pudding mix.

Peanut Butter
Cupcakes

1 white cake mix

ingredients listed on back of box

½ cup creamy or chunky peanut butter

1 cup peanut butter baking chips

Frosting

¼ cup creamy peanut butter

1 container (6 ounces) vanilla yogurt

1 container (8 ounces) frozen whipped topping, thawed

chopped Reese's cups

Preheat oven to 350 degrees. In a large bowl, prepare cake mix according to package directions. Beat ½ cup peanut butter into the batter with an electric mixer. Stir in peanut butter chips. Line two 12-cup muffin pans with cupcake liners. Fill each cup with 3 tablespoons of cake batter. Bake for 20–24 minutes. Allow cupcakes to cool.

In a separate large bowl, whisk together ¼ cup peanut butter and yogurt until smooth. Fold whipped topping into the yogurt mixture. Frost individual cupcakes and refrigerate until ready to serve. Decorate with Reese's cups.

Glazed Cherry Chippers

1 cherry chip cake mix
2 eggs
$\frac{1}{3}$ cup canola oil
$\frac{3}{4}$ cup water

Glaze
1 tablespoon butter or margarine
$1\frac{1}{2}$ cups powdered sugar
$2\frac{1}{2}$ tablespoons milk
$\frac{1}{8}$ teaspoon salt
$\frac{1}{4}$ teaspoon vanilla

Preheat oven to 350 degrees. In a large bowl, combine cake mix, eggs, oil, and water until smooth. Prepare a mini muffin pan with nonstick cooking spray. Place 1 heaping tablespoon batter into each cup. Bake for 10–12 minutes until golden around edges. Allow to cool for 5 minutes before removing to cooling rack where the cupcakes can completely cool. Repeat with remaining batter.

To make glaze; melt butter for 10 seconds in a medium microwaveable bowl. Stir in powdered sugar, milk, salt, and vanilla until smooth. Immediately dip the bottoms of cupcakes into glaze. Allow glaze to drizzle off cupcakes until just lightly coated. Place mini cupcakes top side down on a platter. Allow glaze to harden before serving.

VARIATIONS: Lemon, orange, pineapple, strawberry, or confetti cake mixes can be used in place of the cherry chip cake mix.

Tart Lemonade
Cupcakes

1 lemon cake mix
ingredients listed on
  back of box
1 envelope (.23 ounce)
  lemonade Kool-Aid
  mix

Topping
4½ cups powdered sugar

½ cup butter or marga-
  rine, softened
4 tablespoons milk
½ envelope (.23 ounce)
  lemonade Kool-Aid
  mix*
½ teaspoon vanilla
yellow or white sprinkles

Preheat oven to 350 degrees. Prepare cake mix according to
package directions and add contents of 1 Kool-Aid mix. Line
two 12-cup muffin pans with cupcake liners. Fill each cup with
3 tablespoons of cake batter. Bake for 20–24 minutes. Allow
cupcakes to cool.

To make the topping; beat powdered sugar, butter, milk, and
second Kool-Aid mix in a separate large bowl. Stir in vanilla. If
frosting is too thick, add 1 to 2 tablespoons milk. Frost cooled
cupcakes and decorate with sprinkles.

**If you would like frosting to have a tarter lemon taste, add more of
remaining Kool-Aid mix to the frosting.*

Bumbleberry Cupcakes

1 white cake mix
ingredients listed on the
    back of box
1 container (6–8 ounces)
    boysenberry or
    blueberry yogurt

Topping
1 container (8 ounces)
    whipped topping,
    thawed
1 container (6–8 ounces)
    boysenberry or
    blueberry yogurt
24 raspberries

Preheat oven to 350 degrees. Prepare cake mix according to package directions. Gently stir in yogurt. Spoon 3 tablespoons batter into each cup of two 12-cup muffin pans lined with cupcake liners. Bake for 18–22 minutes until golden brown. Allow to cool 5 minutes before removing from pan.

After cupcakes have completely cooled, using a large bowl, gently fold whipped topping into yogurt. Frost cupcakes with topping and decorate with raspberries.

Candy-Coated
Ice Cream Sandwiches

MAKES 12 ICE CREAM SANDWICHES

½ cup butter or
  margarine

1 chocolate cake mix

2 eggs

vanilla or chocolate ice
  cream

1 package (10–12 ounces)
  mini M&Ms or Reese's
  Pieces

Preheat oven to 350 degrees. Melt butter in a large microwaveable bowl in the microwave for 30 seconds. Stir until most of the butter is melted. Pour cake mix over butter. Make an indentation in the middle of the cake mix and add eggs. Stir until dough forms. Using a 2-tablespoon-size cookie scoop, drop balls of dough onto a baking sheet that has been prepared with nonstick cooking spray. Bake for 12–14 minutes. Allow cookies to completely cool on the sheet.

Place a large scoop of ice cream in between 2 cookies. Press cookies into ice cream until ice cream reaches the edges of the cookies. Place candies in a medium bowl. Roll each ice cream sandwich in candies. Individually wrap each ice cream sandwich in clear plastic wrap. Place sandwiches in an airtight container and freeze until ready to serve.

Sandy Beach
Buckets

1 yellow cake mix

ingredients listed on
back of box

1 package (8 ounces)
cream cheese, softened

3½ cups milk, divided

2 boxes (3 ounces each)
vanilla instant pudding

1 container (8 ounces)
whipped topping,
thawed

½ package vanilla sand-
wich cookies

gummy sea creatures
or fish

Prepare and bake cake according to directions on package box, then cool. Crumble cake into 1 large or 2 medium new and washed sand buckets. In a large bowl, mix cream cheese until smooth. Stir in ½ cup milk until combined. Add remaining 3 cups milk and pudding mixes, blending until thickened. Gently fold whipped topping into pudding mixture. Spoon the pudding mixture on top of cake crumbs. Crush cookies and place them on top of pudding mixture. Refrigerate leftovers. Decorate with gummy sea creatures or fish.

VARIATION: You can make individual-size servings by using small sand buckets.

Red, White, and Blue
Cake

1 white cake mix

ingredients listed on back of box

1 cup boiling water

2 boxes (3 ounces each) berry blue gelatin mix

1½ cups lemon-lime carbonated soda

1 box (3 ounces) instant cheesecake or vanilla pudding mix

1½ cups milk

1 container (8 ounces) frozen whipped topping, thawed

sliced strawberries or raspberries

Prepare cake mix and bake according to directions on package in a 9 x 13-inch pan that has been prepared with nonstick cooking spray. Using a fork, carefully poke holes all over cake while it is still hot. Place water in a large bowl and whisk in gelatin until it is completely dissolved. Then whisk in lemon-lime soda. Pour gelatin mixture evenly over the cake. Cool cake completely and refrigerate for 5 hours or overnight.

Whisk together pudding mix and milk until thick. Spread evenly over cake and frost with whipped topping. Decorate the top with sliced strawberries or raspberries.

VARIATION: Use raspberry or strawberry gelatin in place of berry blue gelatin. Garnish with blueberries instead of strawberries or raspberries.

Cutesy Cobbler

3 cups mini marshmallows

1 yellow or white cake mix

1 can (29 ounces) sliced peaches, with syrup

vanilla ice cream or whipped cream

Preheat oven to 350 degrees. Place marshmallows evenly over the bottom of a 9 x 13-inch pan that has been prepared with nonstick cooking spray. Sprinkle 1/2 of cake mix evenly over top of marshmallows. Spoon peaches evenly over top of cake mix and then sprinkle remaining cake mix evenly over peaches. Drizzle remaining syrup evenly over the top. Bake for 50–60 minutes until golden brown. Serve warm with a scoop of ice cream or whipped cream over individual servings.

Ice Cream
Cupcake Bites

MAKES 80–84 ICE CREAM CUPCAKE BITES

1 cake mix, flavor of choice*

ingredients listed on back of box

ice cream, flavor of choice*

powdered sugar

Preheat oven to 350 degrees. Prepare cake mix according to directions on box. Prepare mini muffin pan with nonstick cooking spray. Place 1 tablespoon batter into each cup. Bake for 10–12 minutes until golden around edges. Allow to cool for 5 minutes before removing to a cooling rack where the cupcakes can completely cool. Repeat with remaining batter.

Slice each cupcake in half and sandwich 1 tablespoon ice cream in between the top and bottom. Place ice cream cupcake bites on baking sheets and freeze for 1 hour or until hard. Individually wrap each cupcake bite in small squares of plastic wrap and freeze until ready to serve. Decorate with powdered sugar before serving, if desired.

CAKE MIX FLAVORS*
* Chocolate

* Spice or carrot
* Lemon
* Strawberry

ICE CREAM FLAVORS*
* Fudge brownie, mint chocolate, or cookies-and-cream
* Dulce de leche, vanilla, butter pecan
* Vanilla
* Strawberry cheesecake, strawberry, or vanilla

Fruity
Pizzas

½ cup butter or margarine

1 white cake mix

1 egg

½ cup flour

¼ cup powdered sugar

1 package (8 ounces) cream cheese, softened

1 container (8 ounces) whipped topping, thawed

1 can (8 ounces) pineapple chunks, drained

1 can (11 ounces) mandarin oranges, drained

sliced strawberries

raspberries

Preheat oven to 350 degrees. Melt butter in a large microwaveable bowl in the microwave for 30 seconds. Stir until most of the butter is melted. Pour cake mix over butter. Make an indentation in the middle and add egg. Stir until dough forms. Mix in flour, working into the dough by hand if needed. Divide dough into 10 equal-size balls. With a rolling pin, flatten each ball into a round circle about ⅓-inch thick. Place 5 circles of dough per baking sheet that has been prepared with nonstick cooking spray. Bake for 10–12 minutes. Allow cookie crusts to cool.

Mix powdered sugar, cream cheese, and whipped topping together. Spread over individual cookie crusts. Top individual pizzas with fruit as desired.

Mini Cheesecake Cups

½ cup butter or margarine

1 white or yellow cake mix

5 eggs, divided

4 packages (8 ounces each) cream cheese, softened

1¼ cup sugar

2 teaspoons vanilla

cherry or strawberry pie filling

Preheat oven to 350 degrees. Melt butter in a large microwaveable bowl in the microwave for 30 seconds. Stir until most of the butter is melted. Pour cake mix over butter. Make an indentation in the middle and add 1 egg. Stir until dough forms.

Line two 12-cup and one 6-cup muffin pans with cupcake liners. Drop one tablespoon dough into each muffin cup. Flatten each ball to form a flat-bottom crust. You will have leftover dough.

In a large bowl, mix together cream cheese, sugar, vanilla, and remaining eggs until completely smooth. Scoop 3 tablespoons of cream cheese mixture over each crust. Bake for 30–35 minutes. Allow to cool. Top individual cheesecake cups with pie filling.

Note: Remaining dough can be made into cookies. Drop small balls of dough onto a baking sheet. Bake at 350 degrees for 8–12 minutes.

Delicious
Cake Balls

1 lemon, strawberry, or chocolate cake mix

ingredients listed on back of box

1 container (16 ounces) cream cheese frosting

1 package (20 ounces) chocolate or vanilla almond bark

1 teaspoon canola oil

candy sprinkles

Prepare cake mix according to directions on package, bake in a 9 x 13-inch pan that has been prepared with nonstick cooking spray, and cool. Crumble cake into a large bowl. Work frosting into crumbled cake until doughy. Line baking sheets with wax paper. Using a 2-tablespoon-size cookie scoop, drop balls of dough onto baking sheets. Freeze cake balls for 2–3 hours.

In a double boiler or slow cooker, melt the almond bark, stirring constantly. Stir in oil. Working with 1 baking sheet of balls from the freezer at a time, use a toothpick or a fork to dip balls in melted almond bark. Decorate with candy sprinkles and place on wax paper where they can harden.

Pumpkin Spice
Muffins

1 spice cake mix

1 can (15 ounces) pumpkin

1/4 cup water

1 container (16 ounces) cream cheese frosting

fall-color sprinkles

candy pumpkins

Preheat oven to 350 degrees. In a large bowl, combine cake mix, pumpkin, and water. Line one 12-cup muffin pan with cupcake liners. Fill each cup 3/4 full and bake for 18–22 minutes. Remove from oven and let cool.

Frost muffins with cream cheese frosting and decorate with fall-color sprinkles and a candy pumpkin.

VARIATION: Muffins are delicious left undecorated if you need a quick treat.

Tangy and Twisted
Trifle

MAKES 12–15 SERVINGS

1 lemon or orange cake mix

ingredients listed on back of box

1 can (14 ounces) sweetened condensed milk

1 container (6 ounces) lemon yogurt

⅓ cup lemon juice

1 container (8 ounces) whipped topping, thawed

1 can (15 ounces) mandarin oranges, drained

Prepare cake mix according to directions on package. Bake in a 9 x 13-inch pan. Allow cake to completely cool.

In a large bowl, combine milk, yogurt, and lemon juice until smooth. Gently fold whipped topping into milk mixture.

Cut the cake into cubes. Place half the cubes into bottom of a large glass bowl. Spread half the whipped topping mixture over cubes. Place remaining cake cubes over top. Frost with remaining whipped topping mixture and top with mandarin oranges.

VARIATION: You can also arrange the cake and topping in individual serving glasses, as pictured.

Happy Everything
Cake

MAKES 15–18 SERVINGS

4 eggs

½ cup canola oil

1 cup water

2 teaspoons vanilla

1 vanilla or white cake mix

1 box (3 ounces) instant vanilla pudding mix

Frosting

½ cup butter or margarine, softened

2 cups powdered sugar

1½ tablespoons milk

1 teaspoon vanilla

Preheat oven to 350 degrees. In a large bowl, beat together eggs, oil, water, and vanilla until smooth. Slowly add in cake and pudding mixes until smooth. Mix for 2–3 minutes. Pour batter into a 9 x 13-inch pan prepared with nonstick cooking spray. Bake for 35–40 minutes until golden. Cool cake completely. Cake can be inverted onto a tray or decorated directly in the pan.

To make the frosting; beat butter with an electric mixer in a large bowl. Slowly mix in powdered sugar and milk until smooth. Stir in vanilla. Spread frosting over cooled cake. Decorate with edible hearts for Valentine's Day; green leaf clovers for St. Patrick's Day; bunnies or decorated eggs for Easter; flags for the Fourth of July; candy pumpkins for Halloween; turkeys for Thanksgiving; or Christmas trees for Christmas.

Berry Sweet
Cupcakes

1 bag (12 ounces) frozen raspberries

1 white cake mix

1 box (3 ounces) raspberry gelatin mix

4 eggs

½ cup canola oil

¼ cup water

1 container (12 ounces) whipped cream cheese or vanilla frosting

red food coloring

pink, white, and/or silver candy decorating balls

Place the frozen berries in a large bowl and allow to thaw for 1–2 hours. Do not drain.

Preheat oven to 350 degrees. In a large bowl, combine cake mix and gelatin mix. Add eggs, oil, water, and raspberries with liquid. With an electric mixer, beat until batter is blended. Line two 12-cup muffin pans with cupcake liners. Fill each cup with 3 tablespoons of cake batter. Bake for 18–22 minutes. Allow cupcakes to cool.

Add 3 to 4 drops of red food coloring to frosting until it reaches the desired color of pink. Frost cooled cupcakes and decorate with candy decorating balls.

Candy Cane
Cupcakes

1 white cake mix
1¼ cup water
2 eggs
⅓ cup canola oil
¾ cup crushed pepper-
    mint candy canes

Topping
1 container (16 ounces)
    vanilla frosting
¼ cup crushed pepper-
    mint candy canes

Preheat oven to 350 degrees. Beat cake mix, water, eggs, and oil together for 2 minutes. Stir in ¾ cup candy. Line two 12-cup muffin pans with cupcake liners. Fill each cup ⅔ full. Bake for 18–22 minutes until golden brown on top. Allow cupcakes to cool and then frost. Decorate each cupcake with ½ teaspoon crushed peppermint candy.

Dreamy Strawberry Cake

1 French vanilla or white
cake mix

1 box (3 ounces) straw-
berry gelatin mix

½ cup canola oil

3 eggs

1 cup sour cream

½ cup buttermilk

1 cup frozen strawberries,
thawed and mashed

1 container (16 ounces)
frozen whipped top-
ping, thawed

sliced strawberries

Preheat oven to 350 degrees. In a large bowl, stir together cake and gelatin mixes. Add oil, eggs, sour cream, buttermilk, and strawberries with liquid. Using an electric mixer, beat all the ingredients together until they are blended. Pour batter evenly between two 8-inch round cake pans prepared with nonstick cooking spray. Bake for 32–36 minutes. Allow cakes to cool completely.

Invert one cake onto a round platter. Frost a layer of whipped topping over the top of cake. Place the other cake on top. Frost top and sides of cake with desired amount of whipped topping. Decorate the top with sliced strawberries.

Butterscotch Sheet Cake

1 box (3 ounces) instant butterscotch pudding mix

2 cups milk

1 yellow or white cake mix

2 eggs

1 cup butterscotch chips

1 teaspoon flour

Frosting

½ cup butter or margarine, softened

3 cups powdered sugar

1 teaspoon vanilla

¼ cup milk

½ cup Heath toffee bits

Preheat oven to 350 degrees. In a large bowl, mix together pudding mix and milk according to package directions. Chill for 5 minutes. Stir cake mix and eggs into the pudding. In a ziplock bag, combine butterscotch chips and flour. Shake the bag to coat. Stir coated butterscotch chips into batter. Spread batter onto a baking sheet with sides that has been prepared with nonstick cooking spray. Bake for 20 minutes. Allow cake to cool.

In a large bowl, beat butter with an electric mixer. Slowly mix in powdered sugar and vanilla. Add milk and beat until smooth. Spread frosting evenly over cake and sprinkle with toffee bits.

Citrus Bundt Cake

1 white cake mix

1 box (3.4 ounces) instant lemon pudding mix

¾ cup orange juice

½ cup canola oil

4 eggs

1 teaspoon lemon extract

Glaze

2 tablespoons butter or margarine

1½ cups powdered sugar

2 tablespoons orange juice

Preheat oven to 325 degrees. Lightly coat the bottom and sides of a Bundt pan with shortening. Lightly sprinkle a small amount of flour over the greased pan. Dump out any excess flour.

In a large bowl, stir together cake and pudding mixes. Pour ¾ cup orange juice and oil over the center of mixes. Add eggs and lemon extract. Using an electric mixer, beat on low speed until batter forms. Increase to medium speed and mix for 2 minutes. Pour batter into pan and evenly spread.

Bake for 45–50 minutes until done. Let the cake cool in the pan for 10 minutes before inverting onto a platter.

To make the glaze; melt butter in a microwaveable bowl for 20 seconds. Stir in powdered sugar and orange juice and mix until smooth. Drizzle glaze over cake.

Fall Harvest Cake

1 butter pecan or carrot
cake mix

2 eggs

1 can (15 ounces)
pumpkin

1 cup white chocolate
chips

Frosting

2 packages (8 ounces
each) cream cheese,
softened

1/2 cup butter or marga-
rine, softened

1 teaspoon vanilla

3 cups sifted powdered
sugar

Preheat oven to 350 degrees. Mix together cake mix, eggs, and pumpkin in a large bowl until blended. Stir in white chocolate chips. Spread batter into a 9 x 13-inch pan prepared with nonstick cooking spray. Bake for 25–30 minutes. Allow cake to cool completely.

In a large mixing bowl, beat together the cream cheese, butter, and vanilla until creamy. Mix in powdered sugar 1/2 cup at a time. Frost the cake with cream cheese frosting. Store in the refrigerator until ready to serve.

VARIATION: A spice cake mix can also be used in this recipe.

Yummy Chocolate Cake

1 chocolate cake mix, any variety
ingredients listed on back of box

Topping
$\frac{1}{2}$ cup butter or margarine

$\frac{1}{2}$ cup water
$1\frac{1}{2}$ cups milk chocolate chips
1 cup semisweet chocolate chips
$1\frac{1}{4}$ cup creamy peanut butter

Prepare and bake cake mix in a 9 x 13-inch pan according to package directions. Allow the cake to cool for 10 minutes. Use the handle of a wooden spoon to poke big holes all over the cake, penetrating to the bottom of the cake.

In a large saucepan, melt butter in water over medium heat. Add chocolate chips and stir until chocolate melts. Stir in peanut butter until it is melted into the chocolate. Pour the chocolate mixture evenly over the cake, allowing chocolate to fall into holes. Spread chocolate evenly over top. Allow chocolate to cool for 10 minutes. Serve this cake warm or refrigerate the cake for 3 hours before serving to allow the chocolate topping to harden.

RICH CHOCOLATE VARIATION: For a richer chocolate flavor, stir 1 cup chocolate chips into cake batter before baking.

Luscious Lemon Cake

4 eggs

$\frac{1}{2}$ cup canola oil

1 cup water

1 lemon cake mix

1 box (3 ounces) lemon
flavored gelatin mix

Topping

1 cup milk

$\frac{1}{2}$ teaspoon lemon extract

1 box (3.4 ounces) instant
lemon pudding mix

1 container (8 ounces)
frozen whipped top-
ping, thawed

fresh raspberries

Preheat oven to 350 degrees. In a large bowl, beat together eggs, oil, and water until smooth. In a separate large bowl, combine cake and gelatin mixes. Using an electric mixer, slowly combine the egg mixture into the cake mix mixture until smooth. Beat on low speed for 1 minute until blended. Increase speed to medium and beat for 4 minutes. Pour batter into a 9 x 13-inch pan prepared with nonstick cooking spray. Bake for 30–45 minutes until golden. Cool cake completely. Cake can be inverted onto a tray or decorated directly in the pan.

In a large bowl, combine milk and lemon extract. Whisk in pudding mix until smooth. Fold whipped topping into pudding and spread evenly over cake. Garnish with raspberries.

Cinnamon Breakfast
Cake

4 eggs

$^1/_2$ cup canola oil

$^1/_4$ cup water

1 cup plain yogurt or sour cream

1 yellow or butter pecan cake mix

$^1/_2$ cup brown sugar

2 teaspoons cinnamon

Glaze

4 ounces cream cheese, softened

2 tablespoons butter or margarine, softened

1$^1/_2$ cups powdered sugar

$^1/_2$ teaspoon vanilla

1 tablespoon milk

pinch of salt

Preheat oven to 325 degrees. In a large bowl, mix together eggs, oil, water, and yogurt until smooth. Add cake mix and beat until large lumps are gone. Pour $^1/_2$ of the batter into a Bundt pan that has been prepared with nonstick cooking spray.

In a small bowl, combine brown sugar and cinnamon. Sprinkle $^1/_2$ the sugar mixture evenly over batter. Top with remaining batter and sprinkle remaining sugar mixture over the top. Run a butter knife in a zigzag pattern though the batter to swirl the cinnamon. Bake for 45–50 minutes. Let cake cool in the pan for 10 minutes.

To make the glaze; beat cream cheese and butter until smooth. Slowly mix in remaining ingredients. Drizzle glaze over cake.

About the Author

Stephanie Ashcraft, author of *101 Things to Do with a Cake Mix,* along with fifteen other culinary offerings, has taught cooking classes based on the tips and meals in her cookbooks for over 13 years. She and her cookbooks have been featured on television and radio stations across the country.

Stephanie is always searching for ways to save time and money in the kitchen and she loves helping others to do the same. She has earned "Favorite Neighbor" status by sharing her culinary creations with those around her. She lives in Tucson, Arizona, with her husband and four children.

Metric Conversion Chart

Volume Measurements		Weight Measurements		Temperature Conversion	
U.S.	Metric	U.S.	Metric	Fahrenheit	Celsius
1 teaspoon	5 ml	½ ounce	15 g	250	120
1 tablespoon	15 ml	1 ounce	30 g	300	150
¼ cup	60 ml	3 ounces	90 g	325	160
⅓ cup	75 ml	4 ounces	115 g	350	180
½ cup	125 ml	8 ounces	225 g	375	190
⅔ cup	150 ml	12 ounces	350 g	400	200
¾ cup	175 ml	1 pound	450 g	425	220
1 cup	250 ml	2¼ pounds	1 kg	450	230